ALCMAEON IN CORINTH

Colin Teevan

ALCMAEON IN CORINTH

after a fragment of Euripides

first perfromed as
COCK OF THE NORTH

Introduction by Edith Hall

OBERON BOOKS
LONDON

WWW.OBERONBOOKS.COM

First published in 2004 by Oberon Books Ltd.
(incorporating Absolute Classics)
521 Caledonian Road, London N7 9RH
Tel: +44 (0) 20 7607 3637 / Fax: +44 (0) 20 7607 3629
e-mail: info@oberonbooks.com
www.oberonbooks.com

A catalogue record for this book is available from the British
Library.

PB ISBN: 9781840024852
E ISBN: 9781786822260

Cover design: Oberon Books

for Madeline

My grateful thanks to Northumbria Live Academy and Live Theatre; to the Department of English at University of Newcastle Upon Tyne, Department of Classics and Ancient History at the University of Durham and Arts Council North East who supported me as North Eastern Literary Fellow; to Madeline Dewhurst, Rosamund Wilks, Joe Phillips, Sunila Gallipatti, Ruth Paton, Mick Sands, the Academy students and most particularly to Martin Wylde who gave me the opportunity to pursue this unique project and Edith Hall who first drew my attention to the fragments, for all their help and encouragement throughout.

Contents

Introduction, 9

ALCMAEON IN CORINTH, 17

Introduction

IN THIS DYNAMIC PLAY, Colin Teevan brings a new form of expression to his longstanding fascination with the ancient Greek dramatist Euripides. Although *Alcmaeon in Corinth* is wholly original, it is inspired by a Euripidean tragedy whose text did not survive the millennia separating us from classical Athens. The pagan schoolteachers and Christian monks who copied out ancient texts, thus transmitting them to posterity, preferred certain kinds of plays to others: not one of Euripides' plays centring on incest survived the selection process. One of these was his *Oedipus*; another was his scandalous *Aeolus*, in which the portrayal of sibling incest was imitated by Ovid in his *Heroides* (no. 11), the direct ancestor of John Ford's *'Tis Pity She's a Whore*. Yet it was (averted) incest between father and daughter that seems to have featured in Euripides' *Alcmaeon in Corinth*. The loss of this tragedy is painful because it was first performed in a group of three, the jam in the sandwich between two extant plays acclaimed as masterpieces, *Iphigeneia in Aulis* and *Bacchae*. Teevan has previously translated both of these for performance.[1] In *Iphigeneia*, Agamemnon has his daughter sacrificed; in *Bacchae* a mother, Agave, slaughters her son. In the missing middle play a father, Alcmaeon, unwittingly acquired his long-lost daughter as a slave. Parenthood and its discontents formed a thread running though the trilogy.

Alcmaeon in Corinth was influential in Greco-Roman antiquity. Aristotle paid it an indirect compliment in his *Poetics* by recommending Alcmaeon (along with the familiar Oedipus and Orestes) in his list of ideal tragic heroes (ch. 13). Lost tragedies named after Alcmaeon were written by the fourth-century Greek Astydamas and the republican Roman poet Ennius. Yet the play published here is an original tragicomedy (or, better, a tragedy sometimes articulated in a comic register). It would have been impossible for Teevan actually to 'reconstruct' the original play,

---

1 *Iph... Euripides, a new version of Iphigeneia in Aulis* (Oberon Books, London, 2002); *Bacchai, Euripides, a new translation* (Oberon Books, London 2002).

since neither a single scene, nor even a list of characters has survived. Although over the last decade Teevan has immersed himself in Greek literature, nobody can know how Euripides himself would have written this play.

The barest outlines of the story were recorded in a Greek mythological handbook, written under the Roman Empire in the first or second centuries AD. Apollodorus' *Library* (3.7.7) says that Alcmaeon's relationship with Manto produced two children, Amphilochus and Tisiphone, whom he left in Corinth for Creon to bring up. Creon's wife sold the girl into slavery, because she was afraid that her husband would marry her; Alcmaeon bought his daughter without realising who she was; at Corinth he retrieved his son Amphilochus as well, who founded Amphilochian Argos.

Teevan's tragedy follows this outline. He produced the script after a triangular discussion in early 2004 with Martin Wylde, the Associate Director of Live Theatre in Newcastle who commissioned it, and myself. It evolved further during a workshop week with the students from Northumbria Live Academy, the actors in the first production.[2] Wylde needed an exciting, substantial piece of contemporary theatre which would stretch his young actors and attract local audiences. But he was keen to experiment with ancient theatrical conventions such as the chorus, and with poetic drama. To me, on the other hand, the appeal lay in re-imagining *Alcmaeon in Corinth* with the help of the surviving evidence. This exercise promised to illuminate *Iphigeneia in Aulis* and *Bacchae*; the protagonist in the first production of *Alcmaeon in Corinth* would, in the preceding play, almost certainly have played Agamemnon, another father wielding undue power over a daughter; in *Bacchae* he would probably have acted Dionysus, the god of drama, who makes a mother kill her son. Such reverberations would have deepened the significance of all three plays.

2 This collaboration between Northumbria University and Live Theatre was established to train postgraduate actors in the North-East, providing the opportunity to commission work on culturally important projects that might not otherwise be immediately commercial.

The relationship between the ancient performances and the post-Renaissance theatre has been one of constant evolution, but the recent wave of interest in fragmentary ancient drama is an exciting – and distinctly postmodern – development. I was intrigued by the transhistorical and ontological status of the fragment, the tiny textual window on a multimedial ancient event; a few words hacked out of both their performance environment and their literary context, to speak – sometimes eloquently – over the centuries. 'Why should people have children, father, if they don't help them in adversity?' was a question someone asked in the original *Alcmaeon in Corinth*; the fragment, which was preserved by an ancient compiler of useful quotations, can be consulted in a dusty work of classical scholarship.[3] But the intense, personal issue it raises provides an excellent example of the creative response that a mere scrap of an ancient playscript can stimulate. Teevan had to decide who would speak these lines, on what occasion, and with what emotional force; in the event the duty of care owed by fathers to their children (which was how he interpreted the fragment) became a structuring principle of his play. Equally, the several fragments about the pollution Alcmaeon incurred through matricide elicited a contemporary interpretation of his problem – a serial adulterer's addiction to sex.

Approximately 23 fragments – perhaps forty lines – have been incorporated into *Alcmaeon in Corinth*. In the absence of any previous English translations of the fragments, I provided some.[4] One seemed particularly comic in its 'take' on kin-murder

3 Fragment 84 in A Nauck, *Tragicorum Graecorum Fragmenta*, second edition revised by B Snell (Georg Olms, Hildesheim: 1964). Many of the fragments of Euripides have never yet been translated into English.

4 And thus ended up, I have been told, as the model for the goddess Hera who recites fragments in the play's prologue. The fragment issue is even further complicated because, three decades earlier, Euripides had dramatised another episode in the same hero's life, entitled *Alcmaeon in Psophis*. This was produced in 438 BCE in the same group as the surviving *Alcestis* and two other lost tragedies (the order was *Cretan Women, Alcmaeon in Psophis, Telephus,* and *Alcestis*). Several fragments used by Teevan could have come from either *Alcmaeon* play.

(fr. 68). Alcmaeon told someone that he had 'killed his mother, to put it in a nutshell'; his interlocutor responded, 'Was this a consensual act, or were you both reluctant?' The obvious humour of this interchange suggested, early in the writing process, that the drama would be predominantly comic. But other fragments show how important to Euripides' conception of Alcmaeon's life story were suffering, danger, and unremitting sex war. These tough issues gradually came to prevail, and Teevan's hilarious dramatic action evolved into something more bleak and profound. Its genre-subverting tone almost spontaneously came to resemble Euripides' late tragicomedies treating childlessness, longlost babies, mistaken identity, secrets and lies – especially *Ion*. The wistful melancholy of these plays foreshadows the complex emotional nuances of late Shakespearean drama.

Future critics will no doubt detect multifarious influences. Euripides' tragedies were renowned for their beautiful melodies, which he composed himself; in *Alcmaeon in Corinth* Mick Sands' sensuous music (specially commissioned and drawing on eclectic traditions including plain chant, where the melodic line is always subsidiary to the sound of the words) was itself a generative influence. While completing the play Teevan reacted to the impact of the four contrasting musical themes – the 'Cock o' the North' chant, the rhythmic, consolatory weaving song, the dissonant madness theme, and the hymn to sexual desire, whose tonality is Spanish and Moorish. When it comes to socio-sexual habits, from ancient gradations in type of prostitute to the punishment of adultery, scholarly works including James Davidson's splendid *Courtesans and Fishcakes* (HarperCollins, London, 1997) were consulted.

At the play's climax Hera appears *ex machina*, to make intertextual connections like a post-modern novelist; she predicts the plot of Euripides' *Medea*, whose heroine will one day kill King Creon, the adoptive father of Alcmaeon's children.[5] Isthmias' account of the sexually charged suicide of Creusa echoes the servant's messenger speech recounting the death of Heracles' wife

5 Teevan was working on a monologue adaptation of Euripides' *Medea* at the same time as writing *Alcmaeon in Corinth*: his *Medea: the Last Word* was broadcast on BBC Radio 3, July 2004.

in Sophocles' *Trachinian Women*. It is the Aeschylean *Eumenides* that underlies the chorus in *Alcmaeon* where the women sing in the voices of Erinyes persecuting Alcmaeon, the mother-killer: 'Our mother was the ink black night / Born long before the Gods.' The bawdy chorus and the temple prostitution scenes are often reminiscent of the girl power characteristic of Aristophanes' *Lysistrata*, but also draw on the elegant epigrams in honour of successful courtesans written by the woman poet Nossis in Hellenistic Italy. Other influences are less Greek: Shakespeare's use of mixed-sex twins, and Giovanni's defence of incest in '*Tis Pity She's a Whore*. The source of the recurrent lyric 'If the lady wants a baby' is a catchphrase attached to Sid the Sexist in *Viz* and chanted by fans of the Newcastle United football team.

Re-imagining a lost ancient artwork opens up questions about the contemporary 'relevance' of plays conceived long ago. As Marx first argued in *The Eighteenth Brumaire of Louis Napoleon* (1852), and Borges elaborated in his famous essay 'Pierre Menard, Author of the Quixote,'[6] recovering a text written in an earlier period of culture inevitably entails the ideology of the reading or spectating subject outweighing the outdated ideology inherent in the hoary text. When we watch a Greek tragedy we watch it with twenty-first century eyes. We can never know how the original audience of Euripides' *Alcmaeon in Corinth* in 405 BCE would have reacted to a man who had abandoned his children. A mother-murderer who was psychologically tortured by the Erinyes, supernatural agents of revenge for kin murder, could have elicited revulsion or pity. Nor can we know exactly how frank the ancient Greeks would have wanted dramatists to be about the sexual desire potentially felt by fathers towards daughters, an uncomfortable impulse which psychoanalysts today would argue is universal.

These questions matter enormously when a modern theatre company stages a surviving ancient tragedy, where it is possible at least to argue about the different responses of an ancient pagan male and a post-Christian, post-Freudian, post-feminist spectator. But perhaps they do not matter at all when the play,

6 First published in *Ficciones* (Buenos Aires, 1944).

like Teevan's *Alcmaeon in Corinth*, is an entirely new interpretation of an unfamiliar legend. The characters in this drama are not reconstructed ancient Greek roles, but third-millennial women and men, lovers and spouses, sons and daughters, placed under a particular type of theatrical microscope. The laws and social conventions of the ancient Corinth imagined by Teevan may be radically different from those which obtain today, but the *emotional reactions* of his knowing, streetwise Corinthians have been imagined from an unapologetically twenty-first century perspective. How does it *feel* when your husband sleeps with every prostitute in town? How would a secluded teenage aristocrat react to being sold into sexual slavery?

The play, then, is not an exercise in piecing something together, but in plunging into fresh, contemporary dramatic waters from an identifiably ancient Greek diving board. Yet the issue of the opposing claims of nature versus nurture, as well as the recurring questions which Teevan puts about education – can humans *adapt to* unfamiliar roles? can a man *learn* to be good? – were originally Greek, even Socratic. There are features of diction and style which Teevan undeniably shares with Euripides; alternatively, perhaps there is something about Euripides which has helped to shape not only Teevan's fascination with familial relationships, and his exuberant exploitation of formal conventions such as the messenger speech, but his actual language and technique: this is apparent in the sharpness and rapidity of the dialogue, and its pointed, reflective tenor. Certain recurrent images, such as birdsong and weaving, have numerous Euripidean parallels. Certain stylistic features, especially alliteration and stigmatism, are typically Euripidean. So are indignant rhetorical questions, persistent anaphora, enjambement, rhyme used for closure, and the interiorised monologue (Teevan's bitter Creusa thus follows in a tradition first established by Euripides' Medea and Phaedra). The clash of registers – where high poetic diction collides with demotic idiom – often creates the type of jarring contrast for which Euripides was appreciated: Teevan has enjoyed presenting the temple prostitution business in the terminology of modern commerce ('We have a broad customer base', says the High Priestess; her employees must each have 'a unique selling point'; Creon charges 'a leisure levy'). The colloquial language is not always so humorous; Creusa's polemic against men is expressed in the language of women's liberation. The ancient poetry of Greek tragedy may run in deep currents beneath the surface of Teevan's contemporary verse, but his Corinthians are recognisable types for modernity. These Greeks do not sound like gods or superheroes. As Aristotle once said of Euripides, the tribulations his people undergo may be extreme, but they speak like ordinary human beings.

Edith Hall
Leverhulme Professor of Greek Cultural History
(University of Durham)
Co-Director, Archive of Performances of Greek & Roman Drama
(University of Oxford)

Characters

HERA

A CHORUS of Corinthian women

TISIPHONE*

ALCMAEON

ISTHMIAS

CREON

CREUSA

NIKARETE, Priestess of Aphrodite

AMPHILOCHUS*

A CHORUS of hierodoules of Aphrodite who include:
GROUND BEATER
FLUTE GIRL
WATER CLOCK
OBOLE

*The parts of TISIPHONE and AMPHILOCHUS
are played by the same actress.*

This version of *Alcmaeon in Corinth* was first performed as *Cock of the North* at Live Theatre, Newcastle on 15 September 2004, with the following cast:

HERA, Deborah McMullan

TISIPHONE / AMPHILOCUS, Catherine Mac Cabe

ALCMAEON, Andrew Horsley

ISTHMIAS, Emma Roxburgh

CREON, John McMahon

CREUSA, Emma-Louise Whittle

NIKARETE, PRIESTESS OF APHRODITE, Polly Goodwin

GROUND BEATER, Laura Breen

FLUTE GIRL, Ellie Fletcher

WATER CLOCK, Emma Roxburgh

OBOLE, Deborah McMullan

A CHORUS OF CORINTHIAN WOMEN, Members of the Company

Director, Martin Wylde

Composer and Musical Director, Mick Sands

Production Designer, Ruth Paton

Movement Director, Tracy Gillman

Lighting Designer, Paul Colley

Live Theatre
7/8 Trinity Chare
Quayside
Newcastle upon Tyne
NE1 3DF

The Goddess HERA in the here and now, sifts fragments.

Hera

'The Gods avenge the pollution
Caused by the murder of a parent'

'Why should people have children, father,
If they don't help them in adversity'

'Aren't you aware, young women,
What's going on in town?'

Fragments, snatches of sentences on dusty leaves
Torn from old book rolls,
Frish-frash fished from the silt of the river
Of two millennia or more of words.

'He destroyed Oedipus
And Oedipus destroyed me,
All because of the golden necklace –'

'In speech I explained that woman is the greatest benefit
And the worst ill for a man to bear.'

'Argaina – becoming white.'

'O child of Creon, how true it is,
That noble children are born of noble men
And children of ignoble men
Resemble their fathers in nature'

So, let us weave these words,
The last stray and fraying threads,
Let us weave them into a fine peplos,
A dress fit for a Goddess. Begin then.

'Friends, young women of Corinth, come see,
A stranger is arriving on the quay.
What sea-girt island is he from?
And why to Corinth has he come?'

Chorus

Corinth, city of the north,
Beloved of Aphrodite,
City of painted temples

And the nightly ecstasies
Of flesh on silky flesh,
The dark mysteries of desire,
Korinthiazomai,
To copulate in the ancient tongue,
Open up your arms in welcome.

Come, women of Corinth,
Angels of the north,
Come from your homes and see,
Sailing back across the years,
Alcmaeon,
Our native son returning,
So leave your weaving and come, come.

Tell, tell of Alcmaeon,
Tell how fearlessly he fought
By his father's side at Thebes.
Tell how his mother, Eriphyle
Bribed with a golden necklace,
Betrayed them to the enemy.
Tell how, over his dying father,
Upon all women he swore revenge,
Most of all upon his mother.
And tell how the oracle then told him
That his mother deserved to die.
But O, as he pushed the knife
Into the belly that had borne him,
His mother cried out
'O, Gods avenge the pollution
Caused by this matricide.
Deny my son shelter, deny him rest,
Let him not find peace on any woman's breast.
Erinyes, avenge my death'

Come women of Corinth,
Angels of the North,
Come from your homes and see,
Sailing back across the years,
The man pursued by the Erinyes,
The kindly ones, lest we too incur their wrath.

So come, women come.

But O the songs that he sang, O,
As he ran from bed to bed,
And O the song that he sang, O,
With those harridans howling in his head.

Nothing is so sweet as desire,
Nectar from the most prized flower,
My mouth overflows with honey.
She who knows not Aphrodite,
Knows not what roses are.

TISIPHONE emerges.

Tisiphone
Excuse me, women of Corinth, but who is he,
Whose boat now draws up to the quay?

Chorus
And who are you? And where've you been?

Tisiphone
Tisiphone, daughter of the king and queen,
Creon and Creusa. I heard the noise
And the excitement, I came down to see
What was happening in the town?

Chorus
Thought you'd see how real women live?

Tisiphone
I didn't mean to be inquisitive, it's just
I know so little of the world, I fear.

Chorus
Sorry Princess, but you're too late. He's here!

Enter ALCMAEON.

Come women of Corinth,
City beloved of Aphrodite,
City of painted temples
And the nightly ecstasies
Of flesh on silky flesh,

The dark mysteries of desire,
Korinthiazomai,
To copulate in the ancient tongue.
Welcome home to Corinth
Alcmaeon.

Alcmaeon

Women of Corinth,
It is gratifying indeed to know
I'm still remembered in my native town,
And to hear my songs still upon the lips,
And such pretty lips I'm bound to say,
Of girls young enough to be my daughters.

Chorus

Listen to how he flatters us.
Can't you just see how he does it?

Tisiphone

Does what?

Chorus

It. Sweeps them off their feet.
What is it, Alcmaeon? What is it brings you home?

Alcmaeon

I'm afraid it's simply business,
Put my affairs in order.

Chorus

His affairs!
Perhaps he has a secret woman here.
Perhaps he is not travelling alone.
Who is she, Alcmaeon? Who is the latest one?

Alcmaeon

You'll be pleased to hear I'm married happily.

Chorus

To wife number three. Or four.
Will there be any more?
Perhaps he's home to find wife number five.

Alcmaeon

I'm sorry to prick your fantasies but –

Chorus

But, will we see you in the market later on?

Alcmaeon

Perhaps when I've seen to affairs of business –

Chorus

You will see to the business of affairs!

Alcmaeon

I will go to the market for a quiet drink.
I think my party years are history.

Chorus

A likely story. The lost years are legendary.
What's it like, Alcmaeon, celebrity?

Alcmaeon

Fame freezes the face at a point in time,
And though inside the man might change,
He is doomed to wear the mask eternally.

Chorus

Did you come direct from Delphi?

Alcmaeon

I now live in Achelous in the west,
But we did stop at Delphi on the way,
To consult with Apollo's oracle.

Chorus

What about? What did the God say?
Was it about the Erinyes – the kindly ones –
We too are kindly ones who follow you – ?

Alcmaeon

What was said was between me and Apollo.
Now, women, my journey has been long –

Chorus

Where are you staying? We'll take you there.

Alcmaeon

The Acrocorinth, I'll find my own way.

Chorus

Some of us, let some of us go with you there –

Alcmaeon

I'm sure that I can remember where –

Chorus

One of us! Choose one of us, Alcmaeon!
Which woman of Corinth do you choose?

Alcmaeon

I can't, you're all so pretty, I really can't.

Chorus

                                        Choose!

Alcmaeon

You then, yes you behind the pillar.

Chorus

                                Her! Her?

But she's not one of us. She's the caterpillar
From the palace, she's no butterfly –

Alcmaeon

You asked me to chose, I've chosen her,

Chorus

She's one of them. Where is the fun – ?

Alcmaeon

I have decided, she's the one.

Chorus

Come women of Corinth,
City beloved of Aphrodite,
City of painted temples
And the nightly ecstasies
Of flesh on silky flesh,
The dark mysteries of desire...

Exit CHORUS.

Alcmaeon

Come out, come on, don't be shy.

Tisiphone

But they'd know the way, better than I.

Alcmaeon

You're not the same as them I can see.

Tisiphone

We are all the same deep down, I believe.

Alcmaeon

You know that killing my mother
Was the source of my celebrity?
Do you still think you're the same as me?

Tisiphone

No.

Alcmaeon

Shame.

Tisiphone

You surely did not mean to cause her harm.

Alcmaeon

And you, you have the most beautiful white arms.

Tisiphone

You try to disarm and deflect with flattery –

Alcmaeon

Did I neglect to ask you your name?

Tisiphone

My mother said not to give my name to strangers.

Alcmaeon

Your mother clearly understands the dangers.

Tisiphone

Sir, I'm afraid I'm sworn to chastity.

Alcmaeon

Not in perpetuity, I hope.

Tisiphone

Nor with a happy heart, but by necessity.
The Acrocorinth is through the gates, up there.
I must leave you to climb the stairs alone.
It is late, my mother expects me home.

Alcmaeon

You walked me, I should –

TISIPHONE is gone.

               – walk you in return.
Of all the pretty heads I've woken to,
Of all the eyes I've kissed open,
And stared into, I swear, hers are the most beguiling.
Smiling, yet knowing, showing herself to me,
Yet hiding, and all the time familiar,
As if the eyes I stared into were my own.
Don't go there, don't entertain such thoughts.
Behind the pretty faces hide the Erinyes,
Alecto, Megaera, and Tisiphone,
My mother's hideous avengers.
I shall see Creusa, retrieve what I require,
Then go home, free from the madness of desire.

Inside the palace.

CREON attended by the servant ISTHMIAS.

Creon

Natural? Natural? What is this natural?
From nature. Yet, are we not made from nature too?
Is man not natural, therefore how can his desires,
Since his desires derive from his own nature,
Be deemed unnatural? More wine, more wine,
It helps loosen the knots tied inside my head.
You are a woman Isthmias,
Is it not natural I desire her?
She is young, she is ripe, her lips, her tongue,
Her breasts, her thighs, as yet untasted
By a boy or man, and from her waking
To her sleeping I am forced to share

The same roof, same table, the same air as her.
Is it any wonder that I suffocate?
Not a word of this goes beyond these walls,
You understand me Isthmias?
We are civilised, we have our rules,
And a man must put his family first,
And it's my own daughter for whom I thirst.
Nor, I fear, are my wife and son, blind to it.
No, I am Creon, King of Corinth,
And I could have my pick of any whore or hetaira
Up in the Temple of Aphrodite,
I must content myself with that.
That's the last you've heard of it, Isthmias.
Now fill my glass.

ISTHMIAS pours.

        Watch out, watch out you ass.
You've overfilled it! The wine's run over,
It's stained, it's stained me, Isthmias.
Damn it, is it not the rules that are unnatural?
Does a dog, a bull, a stallion or a bear
Care for such conventions or civilities?
Or indeed the Gods? Does Zeus care
For the proximity of relationship
To the object of his rapacity?
He married his own sister Hera.
And, as Zeus rules Olympus, I rule here,
I am Creon, King of Corinth
I'll desire whomsoever I want to desire.
I'm burning up, Isthmias. I'm on fire.
Loosen my collar. See how I struggle?
It's as though she squeezed my stomach
In her small white fist, her laughter makes me sweat,
Yet a cold wind blows through my heart,
All at the same time. I can't concentrate.
I pace my study lost, not in affairs of state,
But reveries where I transform into
A dog, a bull, a stallion or a bear,
And have her, Isthmias! O, sweet seduction!

I have Tisiphone, our little gift from Apollo,
The God of healing and destruction.

Isthmias

Creon, your highness?

Creon

What is it, Isthmias?

Isthmias

Your wife Creusa comes.

ISTHMIAS tries to tidy CREON up.

Creon

What's next on official business?

Isthmias

Last quarter's leisure levy
From the Temple of Aphrodite.

Enter CREUSA from interior with a letter.

Creusa

Creon, my husband.

Creon

Creusa, my wife.

Creusa

Creon, have you seen our daughter?

Creon

Seen her? (*Aside.*) O that I had never seen her!

Creusa

What was that, husband?

Creon

I'm sorry, wife, you were saying?

Creusa

Our daughter Tisiphone.

Creon

I know her name.

Creusa

Well?

Creon

Well what? Is she not at home?

Creusa

She went down to the quays some time ago, alone.

Creon

Tisiphone is a big girl now. Isthmias, go on.

ISTHMIAS pours more wine into CREON's cup.

Creusa

That's what worries me, Creon –

Creon

I mean, Creusa, I'm sure she will be fine.

Creusa

And you Creon, have you not had sufficient wine – ?

Creon

Who are you to say when I've had enough – ?

Creusa

Your clothes, look, they are a mess.

Creon

Or, for that matter, tell me how to dress?

Creusa

Your wife, that's who I am, last time I checked.

Creon

Only that because the God Apollo
Conjured from your barren belly
Offspring for me, if not you'd soon see
Your cosy situation spoiled –

Creusa

Of course the fault could never be
With the seed, rather than the soil –

Creon

And as for those children that you bore me –

Creusa

What of them?

Creon

Don't start me on the subject.

Creusa

I won't, on that score, it's *you* bore *me.*

Creon

A boy you told me was this Amphilochus,
A boy who'd one day be a man,
Inherit my title, my name, my land;
Yet he is less a boy, and more a streak of piss;
He is sullen, surly, sulking and spoiled,
He is feckless, faithless and effeminate,
He's not fit to run my bath, let alone the state.
And as for her, for Tisiphone –

Creusa

What about Tisiphone?

Creon

All she cares about is catching glances,
And conferring coy looks, and secret smiles,
She should, she should, I categorically believe –

Creusa

Should what?

Creon

Should stay at home and weave,
Instead of gallivanting round the town,
Men eyeing her – I know how their minds work.
Their filthy, filthy minds –
I tell you, I tell you, I won't stand for it anymore,
I need some air. I am going out.

Creusa

Go then.

Creon

I do not need your permission, wife. Good day.

Exit CREON to exterior.

Creusa

No, you do not need my permission
To do anything, while my position
Hangs by a thread that's yours to dangle or cut down.
So must women weave by other means the web
By which they might preserve their places in this world.
Isthmias, go to the temple of Aphrodite,
Tell the high priestess, Nikarete,
I wish to speak to her immediately.

Exit ISTHMIAS to exterior.

O, my mind is full of knives,
Clashing and clattering in disputation.
I'm cut apart by my desires,
But the main desire must be, Creusa,
To preserve both yours and your children's lives.
Did I not give him what he most desired,
When he returned home from the war at Thebes?
Did I not give him a daughter and a son?
Two children he could call his own?
What matter if they came not from my womb,
Nor the seed from his o-so-royal loins?
We've been mother and father to them both.
Besides, it flattered him to think our twins
Gifts from the twin-born God Apollo.
The God had given him heredity and succession,
While I had ensured my own position,
And for sixteen years we've been a family.
But now that artless, guileless Tisiphone
Grows more captivating daily.
O, I love her, how could I, her mother, not?
I'm proud of her and think her beautiful!
Yet I cannot help but see her youth mocks me,
Her soft white skin scorns the tattered sacking of my face,
Her lightness of touch and tread and humour

Makes me feel mean, shrivelled, old and sunken.
Nor am I blind to him, I know how his mind works.
I know it's only paternal duty
That prevents him from slinging me aside.
What's more the God Apollo prophesied
The first man she ever lay beside would be her father.
I felt I had no option but to tell her,
Horrified she's sworn herself to chastity.
But this now only serves to stimulate his lust,
He finds no relief. And as if that weren't enough
I get this letter; Alcmaeon has come back.
Alcmaeon, hero of the war at Thebes,
Alcmaeon, murderer of his mother,
Alcmaeon, whom I loved like life itself,
Where he sang the song, I danced to his tune,
Alcmaeon, father of our twins by Manto,
The Pythoness of Apollo's shrine at Delphi.
He swore to me sixteen years ago
He'd have no more to do with them.
That was the condition that I took them in
And raised them, his Pythoness's brats.
If his paternity is revealed,
That shall be it, my fate will then be sealed.
Nothing to stop Creon both having Tisiphone,
And having me put to my death.
My only hope lies in keeping Alcmaeon
And his daughter and his son apart,
So for a second time, I must break my heart.

Enter TISIPHONE from exterior.

Creusa

Is that the Priestess of Aphrodite?

Tisiphone

No Mother, it is me.

Creusa

Tisiphone?
It's getting late, where have you been?

Tisiphone

I was helping a stranger find his way.

Creusa

I have told you often not to stray –

Tisiphone

This stranger was nice and kind and charming.

Creusa

They are the most dangerous and disarming.

Tisiphone

And I did feel somewhat disarmed,
As if I knew him from some place else.
But there was no harm in it, mother,
He does not even know my name.

Creusa

All the same, Tisiphone, all the same –

Tisiphone

Mother I have sworn myself to Artemis,
Goddess of chastity, Goddess of the moon,
Though in truth I would walk in the sun
And run around the town, and have some fun,
The way the other girls of Corinth do –

Creusa

Sooner this, than have the oracle come true.

Tisiphone

But what more can I do?

> *ISTHMIAS knocks and enters.*

Isthmias

Nikarete, the Priestess of Aphrodite is here.

Creusa

One moment, Isthmias.

> *Exit ISTHMIAS.*

> Tisiphone, do not fear,

We won't let this oracle destroy your life.

Escorted by the Priestess of Aphrodite,
You will make a trip, a pilgrimage,
To Apollo's oracle at Delphi.
This prophesy about your father
Needs clarifying. Defying one's fate
Is a dangerous occupation,
It brought about Oedipus' ruination.
And don't you worry, Tisiphone,
Amphilochus your brother
Will accompany you too. Go fetch him,
While I talk the details through with the high priestess.

> *TISIPHONE crosses with ISTHMIAS,*
> *who shows NIKARETE in, then leaves.*

Nikarete, you are welcome to the palace.

Nikarete

Thank you Lady Creusa, but to what
Do I owe this unexpected pleasure?

Creusa

Nikarete, you are someone with connections,
Your Temple does business with all sections
Of our Corinthian society.

Nikarete

We have a broad customer base, Lady –

Creusa

There's something I want you to do for me.

Nikarete

Yes, Lady Creusa –

Creusa

I have two slaves, twins, a boy and girl,
Brought to our house as babies by my husband,
Refugees from the war at Thebes they were.
We gave the best to these slave children,
But rather than their gratitude, we've earned
Their resentment. Whatever we might give them
Is never quite enough, they mooch, they moan,
And when they are at home, they do nothing

34

But lounge around like well fed cats.
In fact, I fear they've begun to steal from us.

Nikarete

The training of slaves, at least for domestic duties,
Lies, I'm afraid, beyond my expertise –

Creusa

Perhaps, but you could find them positions
Away from the palace – (*Aside.*) further away the better –
Under a reliable trustworthy master or mistress,
From whom they might learn the obligations
That come with a life of servitude.

Nikarete

Why not take them to the market
If you want them sold as slaves?

Creusa

No, not sold, and my husband must not know.
He's famed for his furious passions.

Nikarete

I know your husband and his passions, well –

Creusa

I've told them that you're taking them
To Apollo's shrine at Delphi,
So they'll go willingly, without a scene,
And my husband not feel obliged to intervene.
Then when the time is right we'll have them back.

Nikarete

And in return for this I receive?

Creusa

The eternal gratitude of the Queen.

> *Enter AMPHILOCHUS from interior.*

Amphilocus

Mother, what's this I hear about a journey?

Creusa

(*To NIKARETE.*) You see, the barefaced audacity!
Amphilochus, this is Nikarete,
She shall escort you on the trip to Delphi.

Nikarete

Twins indeed. Uncanny. Two sides of the same coin.
One the pretty head, and this the tail.
But perhaps there might yet be
Some coins too in this for me.
Stand up straight, boy, and let me see you.

Amphilocus

And who is she, mother, to talk like this to me?

Nikarete

I am Nikarete, priestess of Aphrodite,
And she is the Queen, address her as such.
Don't worry, we'll soon have him sorted out!
Meet me in the market with your sister,
We leave for Delphi within the hour.

Exit NIKARETE.

Amphilocus

Why must I go to Delphi with that woman?

Creusa

Have I not heard you always swear
That you'd protect your sister,
Dare any man lay but a little finger on her?
Well now's your chance.

Amphilocus

But why the sudden need?

Creusa

Tisiphone has just turned sixteen –

Amphilocus

So?

Creusa

The prophecy!

Amphilocus
But our fate is our fate –

Creusa
But perhaps it's not too late to change it.

Amphilocus
It wouldn't be our fate if we could change it!
Is it really the prophecy you fear?
Or the simple fact of our being here?

Creusa
What kind of question is that to ask me?

Amphilocus
I shiver in the shadow of your neglect, mother.
And if you did not protest otherwise,
I would say that you despised my sister.

Creusa
I love her, I love her, she is my child.

Amphilocus
She has turned sixteen and I see clearly
That men's gazes have moved from you to her.
Her looks, natural, her grace, animal,
Not an effigy of youth with a painted face,
But youth itself, mother.
Something in you seeks to see her ruined.

Creusa
Ruined? I would give my life for her.
As for this jealousy you think you see,
She is a mere child, I am a woman,
And you are a peevish little pup.
A real man would know the difference.
Perhaps for once your father's right,
You have been spoiled.
It is good you leave so soon, the time has come,
I must cut the apron strings and set you free,
Or they'll become the web and you the fly.
So, Amphilochus. Good-bye.

Exit CREUSA to interior.

Amphilocus

Yes, mother, I'll make this journey too.
And I swear I'll protect my sister lest you,
Or any of your priestesses, pawns or pimps,
Attempts to touch my dearest, sweetest twin.

Exit AMPHILOCHUS.

Chorus

Secret the cave
And secret the story
Where first Aphrodite
Followed the fire.
She stole from the bed
As the first light was dawning
And into the arms
Of the young God of war.

The flailing, the wailing,
The blood on the floor,
The flesh and the mess
As Desire danced with War.

The all-seeing sun
Had seen her there stealing
And told Hephaestus
With whom his wife lay.
Fired by his fury
At his wife's double-dealing,
He forged a net
To trap them at play.

The flailing, the wailing,
The flesh and the mess,
The laughter of Gods
To see the distress.

Sweet, secret fire,
Flames of destruction,
Where Hephaestus first forged
The necklace of gold.

Circlet of emeralds, which glow with dull fury,

Ominous figures on adamant stamped,
Gorgons eyes gouged from thunderbolt sparks,
Adders heads, serpents crests, all interwoven,
All smithed and tempered, engraved and refined,
So none might suspect the secrets enshrined.

O splendid sun,
See not our secret steps,
Nor where they lead,
Let us stay in your light.
Though let us gasp and gape and laugh,
As the Gods did to see
Others burn in the fire of shame.
Let us not be to blame,
Let us look but not touch,
Let us desire and be desired,
But not too much.

Creusa

Alcmaeon.

Alcmaeon

Creusa.

Creusa

It's been a while.

Alcmaeon

It's been too long.

Creusa

Drink?

Alcmaeon

No. Thank you.

Creusa

I hope you don't mind then if I do.

Alcmaeon

Creusa – ?

Creusa

Yes?

Alcmaeon

    – don't be like this please –

Creusa

Please? Are you now begging me, Alcmaeon,
As once upon a time I begged you?
'Please Alcmaeon, don't leave me please'
You did not answer me.

Alcmaeon

    I did love you.

Creusa

O please! Your love is like the mountain sun,
By day it burns us, our lips crack and we are blinded,
By night, it has disappeared and we freeze.
So don't please 'please' me, please your Pythoness.

Alcmaeon

You know Manto and I finished years ago.

Creusa

So, who's the latest? There's always one.

Alcmaeon

Creusa, I know that I have lost all right
To ask any more of you –

    Creusa

    That's right!

Alcmaeon

Creusa, I'm trying to make amends.

Creusa

So this is the 'I messed up your whole life' speech,
'But can't we still be friends?'
You know the one condition I held you to –

Alcmaeon

Creusa I did not wish to disturb you
Or your domestic tranquillity –

    CREUSA pours another drink.

Creusa

In that case, please get on with it,
Creon could back at any minute.

Alcmaeon

I too have found a measure of contentment,
On the muddy delta of a river
Newly risen from the waters;
A place without history, in the arms –

Creusa

Now I must say, 'O please, Alcmaeon, please!'
Spare me, I've heard it all before.

Alcmaeon

But this time it's different, it's more…
We're married – yes, I know she's the third –
But this time I give my word –

Creusa

You gave your word not to come back –

Alcmaeon

Nor would I, like I said, I had found peace,
Until she, Callirhoe, my wife that is,
Until she demanded, as my true wife,
I get for her a possession of my mother;
The necklace of Harmonia,
Forged by the blacksmith God Hephaestus,
And given by the Goddess Aphrodite
To Harmonia on her wedding day.
It was this same necklace that was used to bribe
My mother to betray my father.
That is why I left it with the children,
Whom I left with you, in your care –

Creusa

Whom you left with me to take care of.

Alcmaeon

– and I know that we agreed I not come back
In later years to try and see them.
I tried to put off Callirhoe, my wife,

But I could not persuade her,
And the Erinyes came flooding back in all their fury.
So I went to Delphi, to ask Apollo what to do,
Who replied that to find true peace of mind,
And earn the respect of my family,
The necklace was the key. That's why I've come to you,
To see them, just the once, to ask for it,
And that will be the last you'll see of me.

Pause.

Creusa

They're not here.

Alcmaeon
Who?

Creusa
Them, the children. Your

children.

Alcmaeon

Where are they then?

Creusa
They are gone.

Alcmaeon
Gone? Gone where?

Somewhere nearby or far across the sea?

Creusa

Across the river.

Alcmaeon
And what river would that be?

Corinth has no rivers –

Creusa
The river Styx.

With Charon in his boat to Hades.

Alcmaeon
But you said you would take care of them.

Creusa

And took care of them I did, Alcmaeon.

Alcmaeon

Took care to be revenged on me, Creusa.

Creusa

Revenge? I came to your rescue.

Alcmaeon

With help like that, who needs bad turns?

Creusa

You did not know which way to turn.

Alcmaeon

I could have murdered them myself.

Creusa

It was murdering your mother made you mad,
Crippled you, caught you forever in the moment.
That's what women see in you;
The little boy in the body of a man.

Alcmaeon

I could have murdered them myself.

Creusa

You could not. You were good for nothing.
'Please Creusa, what am I to do?
Their mother has abandoned them and me.
Look at them, little twin born beams of light.
What kind of father would I be,
With the Erinyes forever singing in my head?'

Alcmaeon

They are never done with me, those kindly ones.

Creusa

And every night a different woman in your bed?
The high price of your celebrity!

Alcmaeon

Pollution more like, all around me dies.

Creusa

– and I told you I would take care of them.
What? Did you think I'd raise your brats as my own?
I have my position to consider,
I am married to this city's leader.

Alcmaeon

I know, Creusa, I was at your wedding.
And are you not forgetting that I fought,
Soon after, with Creon in the war at Thebes.
I saved his life. And, though you'd sworn me to secrecy,
I've always thought that deed part repayment
For the debt that I owed him;
For being the father I could never be to them.

Creusa

Well, you will have to think it otherwise.
Besides, we now have children of our own.

Alcmaeon

I understand, I'd no right to expect you
To care for my children all these years –

Creusa

I would love of course to introduce them,
But I'm afraid our two are out of town –

Alcmaeon

I'm not sure I could bear to meet yours,
When so recently, I have lost my own –

Creusa

Delphi. I'm surprised you didn't meet them there.
There again, perhaps that's for the better –

Alcmaeon

But tell me, please, tell me how and where
It was that you…took care of them?

Creusa

You swore you would not ask after them.

Alcmaeon

That was then. They are my children.
Is it so strange a father wants to know
Where his dead children lie?

Creusa

No.

Alcmaeon

So?

Creusa

A mountainside, is that not how it's done?

Alcmaeon

I don't know, you were the one who did it.
What mountain, where?

Creusa

I cannot say for sure.
It was not me who took them there.

Alcmaeon

Who then?

Creusa

A servant. I could hardly bear
Do such a barbaric thing myself.

Alcmaeon

Which servant? Does he still work for you?

Creusa

She, and it was years ago.
What difference can it make?

Alcmaeon

It will make a difference to my sanity
And to my marriage. The necklace –

Creusa

I'm glad to see your recent pangs of responsibility
Were only temporary, Alcmaeon.
You are just the same as you always were;
Little boy lost, thinking only of yourself.

How grateful would you be, Alcmaeon?
If I could lay hands upon this trinket?

Alcmaeon

Eternally, Creusa.

Creon
(*Singing off.*)

If the lady wants a baby –

Alcmaeon

I'd be grateful eternally.

Creon
(*Singing off.*)

If your meat wants some gravy –

Creusa

Let me see then what I can do.

Creon
(*Singing off.*)

If your 'don't know' needs a maybe –

Creusa

Perhaps I can remember the servant who –

Creon
(*Singing off.*)

Then I'm the cock of the north!

Creusa

– took them to the mountain and perhaps
They can remember where they left them to die.

Enter CREON throwing off coat.

Creon

I was on my way to the citadel –

Creusa

To visit the temple of Aphrodite –

Creon

My evening stroll around my realm,
But found all the streets swelled with women,

Laughing and singing and telling stories.
I asked one of them why they weren't at home
And she said they'd come out for Alcmaeon.
Alcmaeon? My old compadre and comrade in harms?
Soldier, singer and superlative seducer?
Alcmaeon! Old Alcmaeon! The Cock of the North!
Where is he? Where is he? I demanded.
What? You mean that you don't know? They all crowed.
He went to your palace a short while ago.
Hurry home, King Creon, they all said,
Or you'll find him with your wife, in bed.

Creusa

No such luck Creon, you can rest assured –

Creon

With my wife in bed? I said.
Of course, they had a thing when they were young,
Though who didn't have a thing with Alcmaeon?

> *CREON produces a large chilli pepper.*

So I rushed home, radish at the ready.
But I'm glad to say it won't be needed.

Alcmaeon

Creon, King of Corinth, scourge of Thebes –

Creon

Not to be confused with my first cousin;
Creon, King of Thebes and complete cunt!
Alcmaeon, Old Alcmaeon, living and breathing!

> *CREON and ALCMAEON embrace.*

Lock up your daughters, the cock is in town!
Speaking of which has our daughter come down?
Have you been introduced yet to my daughter?

Alcmaeon

I'm afraid I have not yet had the pleasure.

Creon

If you had I'd really have to radish you,
I'd hang you by the bollocks from the bell tower,

If you so much as touched Tisiphone.

Creusa

Creon, please.

Creon

What?

Creusa

Make some effort to hide your jealousies.

Creon

Does not every father think his daughter
Unparalleled in beauty and in grace?

Creusa

You're embarrassing him, look at his face.

Alcmaeon

I'm sorry, it's the name that made me flinch.

Creon

Who? Tisiphone?

Alcmaeon

One of the Erinnyes.

Creon

The kindly ones?

Alcmaeon

Alecto, Megaera and Tisiphone.
Tisiphone means 'revenge for slaughter'.

Creon

Wife? Did you know this when you named our daughter?
Where is she? I want his opinion of her,
He's well known to be a connoisseur.

Creusa

She is not here.

Creon

Where is she, then?

Creusa

She's gone to Delphi with her brother.

Alcmaeon

She has a brother?

Creusa

Yes, he's younger, slightly.
(*Aside.*) Five minutes you once told me, at the most.

Creon

But when did she decide to go?

Creusa

It was planned some time ago.
She wanted to consult the oracle.

Creon

What about?

Creusa

The truth.

Creon

What truth? What is there to know?

Creusa

You know what they're like at that age;
About who she is and what she wants to be.

Creon

She's Tisiphone and she'll surely make
A fine wife for some important man,
And Alcmaeon is just such a man.

Alcmaeon

I thought you said if I so much as touched her –

Creon

Seduction and marriage are quite different affairs.

Creusa

One the promise of plenty, the other a raging thirst.

Creon

Like women, the best thing in life and the worst!

Alcmaeon

Creon, though I can't change the past
I have changed myself.

Creon

                         Of course, of course,
We have all grown wiser as we've grown less able.

Alcmaeon

I had in fact hoped to find my own daughter.

Creusa

(*Aside.*) The longer they stay on this subject –

Creon

You've a daughter in this city too?

Creusa

(*Aside.*) The sooner they shall see –

Creon

I didn't know this, Creusa, did you?

Alcmaeon

No, not any more, she died it seems.

Creon

I'm sorry, I mean, what a pity.

Creusa

(*Aside.*) And the fabric of my family unravel.

Creon

I know, why don't we go out?
I'll show you how the town looks by night

Creusa

Yes do, go out and grab a bite.

Creon

We can catch up, and like she says, have some food.

Alcmaeon

Thank you, Creon, but I'm not in the mood.

Creusa

O yes, Creon, you'll never guess,
Alcmaeon has found wedded bliss.

Creon

That's not hindered him in the past.

Creusa

You two go out and eat and drink,
And I'll stay here and have a think.
I'm sure that I'll remember whom
I gave that thing that was with the thing
That you asked me to take care of to.

Creon

Something I should know, you two?

Creusa

No, just an old memento.
Now, you two go out and have some fun –

Creon

Come on, Alcmaeon, let's go, this is party town.

Exit CREON and ALCMAEON.

Creusa

– while I find out where the necklace has gone;
It must be worth one last dance with Alcmaeon.
Isthmias, come here, I have a job for you.

Chorus

Let us go up to the temple,
To where
The golden statue of Aphrodite stands,
Resplendent, erubescent in the setting sun,
Paid for by the priestess Polyarchis
Who made her fortune
From the splendour of her body.
And there,
Before the business of the night begins,
The hierodoules,
The sacred slaves of Aphrodite,

Weave
A dress fit for the Queen of Heaven.

The weft is woven through the warp,
I push the shuttle back and forth,
My life lies stretched upon a loom,
This house of love shall be my tomb.

Young girls sing songs to Aphrodite,
They see not the reality
Of her child Eros who does not care
Whom he crosses, whom he infects,
Whom he reduces to despair
With his fatal shafts, with sex.
It is he who makes the good man crave
And the man who then makes the woman slave.

The weft is woven through the warp,
I push the shuttle back and forth,
My life lies stretched upon a loom,
This house of love shall be my tomb.

Nor are the Gods immune,
When Eros sings his heady tune;
Zeus fell for Hera, his own sister,
And though she attempted to resist him,
He turned into a small cuckoo
Whom she pitied and pressed to her breast,
Where Zeus retook his male shape
And sang out, cuckoo! cuckoo!

The weft is woven through the warp,
I push the shuttle back and forth,
My life lies stretched upon a loom,
This house of love shall be my tomb.

O, to be free
From the nightly weave
From bed to bed,
And spin my thread
Across the sea,
Far, far away from here,
To be free to follow my own desires.

Hera, Lady,
Hera, Protectress,
You who've suffered indignities,
Yet still stand proud,
Queen of heaven and wife,
Of all-thundering Zeus.
We know the dangers of excess,
Nor do we dress ourselves as Gods.
Receive this gift
From the slaves of your stepdaughter.
It smells of incense and of nectar,
And is woven from the threads of our life.
Hera, hear our prayer.

Enter NIKARETE and TISIPHONE.

Nikarete

This way, this way, this is where you'll stay.

Tisiphone

But I thought we were to go to Delphi.

Nikarete

Well, you were wrong, there's been a change of plan.

Tisiphone

And where did my brother Amphilochus go?

Nikarete

To the High Priest of Apollo for a song.

Tisiphone

But this is the temple of Aphrodite – ?

Nikarete

Through her twelve positions, you shall learn yours.
And these are my daughters, the Goddess' sacred slaves.

Tisiphone

Please to meet you, pleased to meet you all, but –

Nikarete

Ground Beater, Water Clock, Flute Girl and Obole.

Tisiphone

Ground Beater?

Ground Beater

I used to walk the public thoroughfares.

Water Clock

She used to be a public thoroughfare!

Ground Beater

Bit rich, coming from a talking clock.
Come in number fifteen your time is up!

Nikarete

Daughters, please welcome your latest sister.

Tisiphone

Hello, yes, pleased to make your acquaintance,
But I'm sure there has been some mistake –

Nikarete

Each girl here is here only by mistake.

Tisiphone

But I'm the daughter of the King and Queen.

Nikarete

All my girls are royalty, in their own way.

Water Clock

My mother was a Phoenician princess.

Ground Beater

Yes, and my brother was a queen of great repute.

Flute Girl

And Creon always calls me 'most highness'
When I play for him on his royal flute.

Tisiphone

Creon? You can't mean that he comes here?

Ground Beater

He is most regular in his coming.

Obole

We set our Water Clock by him –

Tisiphone
But Creon, the king, he's my father.
Of all the places in all the world –

Ground Beater
Don't worry, child, we're all his little girls.

Tisiphone
But I can prove to you just who I am,
I have a necklace, proof of my identity,
My father won it in the war at Thebes,
The necklace of Harmonia. Look, here.
How could a common slave or hetaira –

Nikarete
A, a,
Language, language, watch what you're saying, dear,
We're all just servants of the Goddess here –

Tisiphone
I'm sorry. I did not mean to offend you,
But you must see that my story's true.

Nikarete
It's a unique piece of work, alright.

Tisiphone
How else could I come by a piece like this?

Nikarete
How indeed? You stole it from the palace!

Tisiphone
No, please, it's mine.

Nikarete
I don't tolerate thieves in this temple,
We have our reputation to protect.

Tisiphone
But my necklace! What will you do with it?

Nikarete
Gold, emeralds, adamant all engraved and embossed…
It will go some way toward redeeming the cost

Of your purchase and funding your freedom.

Tisiphone
My purchase? My freedom? What do you mean?
My mother wanted me to go to Delphi.

Nikarete
How can you maintain she is your mother?
True, she's been generous to you to a fault,
It's a big mistake to indulge one's slaves.
Creusa wanted you retrained elsewhere,
Be thankful I've taken you into my personal care.

Tisiphone
My own mother asked you to sell me?

Nikarete
Creusa! Creusa asked me to save you.

Tisiphone
And my brother too is now a slave?

Nikarete
You nor he were never anything else!

Tisiphone
And he swore he would protect me.

Nikarete
We will protect you. We are now your family.
And we've a family business to run.
Come on, the evening rush is starting soon,
And you're not yet trained in the amorous arts.
And apparently Alcmaeon's in town,
We need to be ready if he calls round.
A man, for once, who knows what he's doing,
When it comes to the ins and outs of screwing.
Besides, think of the publicity
His patronage will bring. So, ladies
We need to be offering a full selection –

Chorus
For the discerning citizens' erections.

Nikarete

Now can you play the kithara or lyre?

TISIPHONE shakes her head.

Or dance, or sing odes or recite speeches?

TISIPHONE shakes her head.

Or be the Goddess of men's fantasies?

Flute Girl

Or satisfy him on your knees!

Nikarete

Flute Girl, please.

Obole

Or from his palm read his mind?

Ground Beater

Or receive him from in front or from behind.

Nikarete

Ladies, whatever your origins might be,
Please remember you are now my daughters;
Train her accordingly, here in your quarters.
She must have a unique selling point.
And I must go and receive the clientele.
So, positions when I sound the bell.

Exit NIKARETE.

Obole

Poor child she doesn't have a clue,
She's no idea what to do.

Ground Beater

I doubt she's ever turned a trick.

Flute Girl

I doubt she's ever seen a prick.

Obole

Can you make your piggy pout?

Ground Beater

Don't trust her, her piggy's got a snout.

Water Clock

She wouldn't know a pimp from a punter.

Tisiphone

Please, please, I am sworn to Artemis the hunter.

Ground Beater

The hunter Artemis?

Flute Girl

She thinks she's better than us.

Water Clock

She thinks she's royalty.

Ground Beater

Must we teach you on a bended knee, Ma'am?

Obole

Perhaps there is an easier way.

Chorus

Making love is like drinking wine,
Some have leisure to take their time,
And swill it round about their mouth,
And pretend they know what they're talking about.
But we haven't got all day,
Our clients pay by the hour,
So here's what you do and what you say.

Dip his finger in the glass
Put it between your lips
And taking care to catch all the drips,
Suck it until it is bone dry.

No, nothing is so sweet as desire,
Nectar from the most prized flower,
My mouth overflows with honey,
She who knows not Aphrodite
Knows not what roses are.

Then lie back and look contented,
As if pleasure had just been invented
And you'd been given the test ride.

So his pride shall swell,
He will think his wine the cause
As his finger droops and falls,
Give his balls a squeeze
And ease him out that door.
Then throw the sediment down the sink,
It's time to pour another drink.

No, nothing is so sweet as desire,
Nectar from the most prized flower,
My mouth overflows with honey,
She who knows not Aphrodite,
Knows not what roses are.

Ground Beater

Remember, we speak in metaphor
For glass read ass, for wine –

Obole

What is the point in a metaphor
If you must explain it, Ground Beater?

Water Clock

But Obole, why must we placate her?

Ground Beater

Just show her the Lion on the Cheese Grater!

Tisiphone

But why would anyone want me?

Obole

How did the Gods seduce human beings?

Water Clock

They transformed themselves into beasts of beauty.

Flute Girl

In that pure form they are irresistible.

Obole

Find the beast or bird most suitable for you, then –

Chorus

Suggest what is beneath but do not show,

Make him beg for more but then say no.
With the right amount of suggestion,
You'll be perfect in his imagination.

No, nothing is so sweet as desire,
Nectar from the most prized flower,
My mouth overflows with honey,
She who knows not Aphrodite,
Knows not what roses are.

> *A bell rings. NIKARETE enters*
> *followed by CREON and ALCMAEON.*

Nikarete
Come through, come through. And, might I just add,
What an honour, Alcmaeon, it is in having you.
Or should that not be you who's having us?

Alcmaeon
Please, Nikarete, don't make a fuss –

Creon
A fuss? At these prices it's us being had.

Nikarete
Creon, you might be king, but you are bad –

Tisiphone
(*Aside.*) Creon, my father? They weren't lying –

Nikarete
You should see the size of his...demands –

Alcmaeon
I thought we'd gone out for a quiet drink –

Nikarete
Tax demands, of course I mean!

Tisiphone
(*Aside.*) And the stranger from this morning on the quay –

Creon
It is the wages, Nikarete, of iniquity.

Tisiphone

(*Aside.*) And what if my father should find me here – ?

Creon

Alcmaeon, make your choice from Korinth's finest.

Tisiphone

(*Aside.*) Or, not recognising me, choose me – ?

Creon

Nikarete's divine daughters.

Tisiphone

(*Aside.*) Is this how my fate is to befall me?

Alcmaeon

I'll just say hello to them, that is all.

Creon

Nonsense, Alcmaeon, it's all taken care of.

Alcmaeon

(*Aside.*) Less taking care of and more care taken
From you or your wife, would not have gone amiss!

Tisiphone

(*Aside.*) O what am I to do Amphilochus?

Nikarete

But why the sullen looks and the long face.

Creon

He thinks himself married happily.

Nikarete

          O Creon,
Is that not what's called an oxymoron?
Happiness in marriage depends upon variety;
That's why my daughters here
Are friends to both you and your wife.
While wives are busy producing sons and heirs
And distracted with domestic cares,
We take care of their mens' physical needs,
While making sure he does not sow his seed
In a field where a rival tree might grow.

Creon

Go on, Alcmaeon, have one for the road.

Nikarete

My daughters cater for all tastes;
Hetairas for the pleasures of the mind,
Pornai to help you physically unwind,
And Aulitrides who'll play for you upon their flutes.

Alcmaeon

(*Aside.*) The Erinyes crawl through my mind
Like scorpions through a dead man's skull.
I am dead, let me stay as I am.

Creon

Besides, it's good for business, good for the renown
Of both the temple and hence, the town,
If they could count you amongst their clientele.
Come on, Alcmaeon, what the hell?
For old times' sake, what do you say?

Tisiphone

(*Aside.*) And what do I say?
I must choose to abandon chastity
And try to be this stranger's fantasy,
Or run the risk of my father choosing me.

Alcmaeon

What harm sing those 'kind ones' in my head?
What harm in one more woman in my bed?
You've had so many, how can one more hurt?

Pause.

What the hell indeed –

Creon

I knew that he'd agree –

Alcmaeon

Line them up then and let me see
How my home town girls compare to the rest.

Nikarete

Girls, if you please, line up for our guests.

Tisiphone

(*Aside.*) O my father, my poor flawed father, it is true
That noble children are born of noble men,
And now, we both together in this place, ignobly,
I see that I am truly born of you.

*The CHORUS and TISIPHONE
are inspected by ALCMAEON.*

Alcmaeon

What of this shy creature in the veil?

Nikarete

A foal as yet unridden by a man.

Creon

And she's said that to every ass
Who's had a ride on her these past two months.

Nikarete

No, I swear to you, she's not been broken in,
She's come directly from a decent home.

Creon

A decent home, and young, I like them young,
Lips and tongue, breasts and thighs as yet untasted,
You've sold her to me, Nikarete,
Tell her to take off her veil, let's see the filly.

TISIPHONE refuses to let CREON look under the veil.

She's a spirited one, and frisky too.
Take off the veil, girl, I am the King.

Nikarete

Take it off, the games are through.

Beat.

Alcmaeon

If she's new to all this, she must be shy.
Perhaps you'd let me have a look and I,
I will describe to them what I have seen.
Please, you have no reason to fear me child.

Tisiphone

(*To ALCMAEON.*)

Swear.

Alcmaeon

I swear.
Give her some space, Creon, she needs some air.

Creon

I would not stand aside for any man,
But you, Alcmaeon, you saved my life.

Alcmaeon

Now child, you are free, lift the veil and let me see.

TISIPHONE raises the veil.

You? I met you this morning on the quay.

Tisiphone

That was another person you met then.

Alcmaeon

And does this new you have a name?

Tisiphone

No. None. Argaina. Becoming white.

Alcmaeon

An ugly sounding name for one so pretty.
What is it you wish to become white?

Tisiphone

The past.

Alcmaeon

Why?

Tisiphone

If we had no memory of happiness,
The present would not seem so sad to us.

Alcmaeon

And why is it that you wear this veil?

Tisiphone

So the past might not see what I've become.

Alcmaeon

And what will this new you do for me?

Tisiphone

I'll transform into a bird for you,
A nightingale blown by the winds
Across the sand and sea from Africa.
Though my voice is weak, I'll sing for you,
And you shall hold me to your breast and stroke me,
And there I shall turn into a woman.

Beat.

Creon

So Alcmaeon, has Corinth tempted you?

Alcmaeon

More than tempted, Creon, I'll have her.

Nikarete

Do you not want one with more experience?

Alcmaeon

No. I've decided, she's the one.

Nikarete

But Clepsydra, the Water Clock,
Has mastered all twelve positions.
And Obole here has seen and done it all.

Alcmaeon

Her, and her alone.

Creon

              I understand, my friend,
The attraction of the unwalked way.
Sometimes I find, you know, with my own daughter,
Sometimes, in her company, I find that I
Can barely breathe. I come here for relief,
But it lasts no longer than my journey home.
Better you have her, don't want to fan the flames.
I'll have Flute Girl here play for me.

Flute Girl

The same old tune?

Creon
The same old tune.

Flute Girl

Come then Creon, come to my room.

Exit CREON and FLUTE GIRL to interior room.

Nikarete

Now, my daughters lead them to their chamber.

Exit ALCMAEON and TISIPHONE
led by the CHORUS.

Enter ISTHMIAS.

Isthmias

Excuse me, madam Nikarete.

Nikarete

Yes?

Isthmias

Isthmias, the servant of Lady Creusa.

Nikarete

I remember.

Isthmias

And I've come regarding a small matter;
The slave that she asked you to sell for her –

Nikarete

That slave is now with her new master.

Isthmias

It's not so much the slave as a golden necklace?

Nikarete

You should have said. Step into my office
I'm sure that I can help you, for the right price.

Exit NIKARETE and ISTHMIAS.

The Bed Chamber.

Enter AMPHILOCHUS.

Amphilocus

So, this is it, the honeymoon suite?
The 'kineteirion' or 'fuck factory'
I've heard it called. I heard it all.
Everything that went on out there.
Better to have no parents than such a pair.
One who'd treat his daughter as his wife,
The other who would exchange the lives
Of her own children to maintain her own position.
I knew that trip was just an excuse
For Creusa to get rid of us.
But this, this is beyond even her.
Selling my sister as a common whore,
And me to the high priest of Apollo.
He told me he admired my pretty face,
And found my lips pleasingly feminine,
Then he took his penis out
And tried to put it in my mouth.
I bit it, then ran for it, I did not look back until
I'd made it all the way up the hill,
To the Temple of Aphrodite,
Where, I swear, I will keep my promise and kill
This stranger when he tries his luck with her.
I shall hide myself behind the bed
And, as he forces himself upon her,
I shall jump up and cut off his head.

He hears the CHORUS coming. He hides. Enter CHORUS.
They work like chamber-maids, turning back the sheets and
leaving an open bottle of wine. ALCMAEON and TISIPHONE
enter. Exit CHORUS.

Alcmaeon

Well, my nightingale, it's just the two of us.

Tisiphone

          Yes.

Beat.

Alcmaeon

Perhaps you'd like a glass of wine?
Samian, I'm afraid, is all they've got.
At these prices, I'd hoped for Chian.

Tisiphone

The Samian's fine. In truth I can't tell
The difference between Samian, Chian or Dodecanesean.

ALCMAEON pours a glass, TISIPHONE gulps it down.

Alcmaeon

Nor will you ever if you gulp it down.
Take your time, put it to your lips, sip.

Tisiphone

I've drunk wine before. I know what to do.
Give me more and I will show you.

ALCMAEON pours her another glass.

Alcmaeon

Show me then what you've learnt since this morning,
For surely then your lips were unstained.

Tisiphone

I've tasted disillusionment since then.

Alcmaeon

You'll know then how to rate this bitter vintage.

Tisiphone

First you raise the glass to admire the tone.

Alcmaeon

What do you see?

Tisiphone

I see a tone that pleases me.

Alcmaeon

But it was grown in harsh sun on twisted vines.

Tisiphone

Its hard experience makes up for the lack of mine.

Alcmaeon

What next?

Tisiphone

Next I move nearer to breathe it in.

Alcmaeon

Breathe what in?

Tisiphone

The body.

Alcmaeon

The body's the thing.

And what do you make of this old dog's scent?

Tisiphone

I find it strangely reminiscent.

Alcmaeon

Of what does it remind you?

Tisiphone

Of vines, of orange blossom and of olive groves,
Of bougainvillea, eucalyptus and geraniums,
Of fig, of pine, of ivy and of oak,
Of dust, of sweat, of laughter and of tears
Of hot dry nights awake staring at the stars,
Of metal on metal, of blood and dust,
Of horses, strange houses, of the road,
The endless, loneliness of the road,
The far from homeness, of never being whole.

Silence.

Alcmaeon

Your tongue and nose are most discerning.

Tisiphone

It's the wine talking, I'm only learning.

Alcmaeon

No, it's you, you must learn to trust yourself.

Tisiphone

Then take his finger and run it round the rim.

Alcmaeon

Why?

Tisiphone

Then dip it in and lick it till it is bone dry –

Alcmaeon

What has that to do with wine?

Tisiphone

That's what the others told me to do.

Alcmaeon

I don't want the others, I want you.

Tisiphone

Then open your mouth and close your eyes –

Alcmaeon

This is not what you want to do.

Tisiphone

I want to do what you want to do,
I know you do. You put it to your lips –

TISIPHONE lifts the wine,

Alcmaeon

No –

TISIPHONE spills the wine on her dress.

It's spilled.

Tisiphone

I've stained my dress.
I'm sorry, I've never done this before.
I feel a fool –

Alcmaeon

I'm going to get you out of those wet things.
What do you need with these silly veils?

TISIPHONE lets him take off her dress.
He does so more like a father than a lover.

Tisiphone

'Suggest what is beneath but do not show.
Make him beg for more but then say no.
With the right amount of suggestion,
Your body will be perfect in his imagination.'

> *Revealed in her underwear, TISIPHONE appears as the*
> *young girl that she is.*

This is not how it's meant to be I'm sure.

Alcmaeon

This is more like the girl I met this morning.

Tisiphone

This morning I was the daughter of a king.

Alcmaeon

Some king to sell his daughter as a whore!

Tisiphone

And some fate to be that daughter.

Alcmaeon

I meant that a father should have more care
Where his children are and what they do.
What right has he to call himself a king,
If he can't take care of the very thing
That is closest and most precious to him?
Who is this so-called king? Where does he rule?

Tisiphone

It is all too close for me to say –

Alcmaeon

Some far-flung, barbarian nation,
Untouched as yet by civilisation.

Tisiphone

I'd rather that my father was further flung,
But I'd rather still be here with you than do
What Apollo's oracle said I'd do.

Alcmaeon

Tell me who he is and where I'll find him?
I'll remind him of a father's duty.

Tisiphone

The faults we find in others are most often
Those we find most monstrous in ourselves.

Alcmaeon

What are you suggesting?

Tisiphone

Nothing. I'm just saying…

Alcmaeon

Saying what?

Tisiphone

You speak as if you had experience.

Alcmaeon

Yes, I am ashamed to say I have.

Tisiphone

Do you have children of your own?

Alcmaeon

Yes. No. I had two. They are gone.

Tisiphone

Excuse me. I did not mean to pry –

ALCMAEON sinks to the floor.

What have I done? What have I said?

Alcmaeon

It's not you, it's the kind ones in my head.

Tisiphone

It's my fault. This is not the talk for bed –

Alcmaeon

They dance, they begin to dance, they link arms –

Tisiphone

Hold me then, hold me in your arms, we'll dance –

Alcmaeon

Your hands, your white hands are clean but mine,
Mine are red with the blood of my mother.
Don't look at me like that.

Tisiphone

Like what?

Alcmaeon

Like her! Like her!

The same dark hair, the same blue eyes.
I must be mad when every girl I meet
Begins to resemble my own mother.

Tisiphone

How could I resemble her? What am I to her, or you?
I'm nothing. Nothing at all.
Here, drink some wine and you'll feel better.

TISIPHONE pours ALCMAEON a drink. He drinks.

Now, it is my job to please you
And, if by pleasing you I calm you,
And defy the fate foretold me,
So much the better. I will make you happy, Alcmaeon.

TISIPHONE drinks again.

What would you like me to do for you?
I've heard of one, the racehorse, do you want that?
I've always wanted to ride but been scared,
To get up upon the back of such a beast –

Alcmaeon

See them dance. See them join hands, they laugh –
Alecto, Megaera and Tisiphone.

Tisiphone

Tisiphone?

Alcmaeon

Revenge for slaughter, it means.

Tisiphone

No, she is dead, Tisiphone's dead.

Alcmaeon

No, she's alive, look at her dance.
You see, you begin to see them?

Tisiphone

Be brave, Tisiphone, be brave.

Alcmaeon

You do, you talk to them, I hear you.

TISIPHONE drinks. She must lie down.

Now see them, see them all sway.
True fury, true justice at play.
The Gods are amateurs compared to these,
This the punishment for the pollution
Of the patricide and matricide.
And now they wake again
At the mention of my dead children.
What? Did I kill them too?
All around me dies.
It is the price of my celebrity.
Look at this girl here;
Abandoned, sold into slavery.
Do you torment her father as you do me?

Chorus

We are the Erinyes,
The forgotten of the world.
Inside your heart
We lie curled and waiting.
To swoop down upon the man
Who takes a knife
To his own family.
We track him down.
He shall run forever,
Dead in life.

Our mother was the ink black night
Born long before the Gods.
We care not for their light,
Nor their ways of winks and nods.
We hunt in the dark,

We hunt to the catch,
We hunt till our staggered, stumbling prey
Begs us to die
Then we say:

Run, crazy head,
Run from bed to bed,
Hide yourself beneath the sheets
Of every little girl you meet,
But do not dare to go to sleep,
Or we shall find you
And fill your mouth and nose with dirt,
And fill your ears with our screeching song.
So run crazy head, run.

We are the Erinyes,
The forgotten of the world.
Inside your heart
We lie curled and waiting.
We snap the strings of harmony,
We screech revenge
Till your ears bleed.
Our pursuit is pitiless,
Our justice never ends.

All men dream of greatness,
All men dream of glory,
All men see themselves
From time to time as Gods.
All dreams die at the point of a knife,
All dreams die in our dark light.
We'll run the rags of hope
Right out of you.

We are the Erinyes,
The forgotten of the world
Inside all your hearts
We lie curled and waiting.
We are the memories of grief
You thought buried,
You thought dead.

Run, crazy head,
Run from bed to bed,
Hide yourself beneath the sheets
Of every little girl you meet.
But do not dare to go to sleep,
Or we shall find you,
And fill your mouth and nose with dirt,
And fill your ears with our screeching song.
So run crazy head, run.

Until you can wake yourself
From the vain dream of your life –

Exit CHORUS.

Alcmaeon
She sleeps. She has drunk herself to sleep,
So she sees not what she feels compelled to do,
Each beast has its means of survival,
And sleep is her armour and…effective too.
I can't. I am unable. Something in me shouts stop.
Is it over? Is this why the oracle
Had me come home? So I might learn restraint,
Responsibility and self-control
In the bed of a Corinthian whore?

*AMPHILOCHUS jumps from his hiding place, grabs
ALCMAEON around the throat, and holds a knife to his neck.*

Amphilocus
That girl's no whore, she's worth more than you or I.

Alcmaeon
Have I not suffered enough?

Amphilocus
You are no victim, Sir, you are the cause.

Alcmaeon
I killed my mother! I killed my mother!
I cannot change it, or make it otherwise.

Amphilocus

I'd not speak so proudly in your position,
Show some humility. What about my sister?

Alcmaeon

What sister?

Amphilocus

My sister, Tisiphone.

Alcmaeon

The old harridan?

Amphilocus

My twin, Tisiphone, lying there!

Alcmaeon

The name must be common then in Corinth,
Creon said he called his girl that too.

Amphilocus

The name's not common, there are less than a few.

Alcmaeon

By that you mean there's only one.
You're saying that she is Creon's child?

Amphilocus

And I am, I'm sad to say, his son.

Alcmaeon

He said I'd find her beautiful, he was right,
Delightful, graceful, charming and true.
All these things, but to find her here?
What kind of father could do that to his child?
He told me that she'd gone to Delphi.

Amphilocus

My mother's excuse to be rid of us.

Alcmaeon

Your mother? Why would Creusa want you gone?

Amphilocus

Envy. She envied all that delights you in my sister,

She feared Creon's feelings for his daughter
Were more than they ought to be.

Alcmaeon
Unnatural man and wife, unnatural family!

Amphilocus
In truth, I never did think us a happy one.

Alcmaeon
But, you said your sister, here, was your twin?

Amphilocus
Did my parents fail to mention me, again?

Alcmaeon
No, Creusa told me that she had a son,
But that he was younger than her daughter.

Amphilocus
What difference does it make if I'm younger
By five minutes or five years?

Alcmaeon
But what age you are?

Amphilocus
Sixteen last spring. What of it?

Alcmaeon
Two sets of twins, both sixteen years of age,
Yet two plus two does not equal four.
I too had twins sixteen years ago
Or the woman I was with then –

Amphilocus
It's coincidence and nothing more.
I hope you were a better father than ours to us.

Alcmaeon
No, I fear I was no better than he was.

> *ALCMAEON searches the still sleeping*
> *TISIPHONE for something.*

Amphilocus

What are you doing? Leave her. Don't touch her!

AMPHILOCHUS pushes ALCMAEON off.
He slumps. He is, in fact, relieved.

Alcmaeon

It's not there, it is not her. You're right
Nothing more than coincidence.

Amphilocus

What is it that is not there?

Alcmaeon

The necklace.

Amphilocus

What necklace?

Alcmaeon

Gold, emeralds, adamant –

Amphilocus

Thief! What have you done with it? Where's it gone?

Alcmaeon

She had a necklace?

Amphilocus

The proof, our mother said, of who we were.
You've robbed us of our identity.

Alcmaeon

Robbed you? I've discovered it, unfortunately.

ALCMAEON pulls away, as he does so his throat is nicked by
AMPHILOCHUS.

The Gods punish in perpetuity
The man who dares to kill his parent.

Amphilocus

Who's killing whose parent? What do you mean?

Alcmaeon

I mean that the sheets of this bed are now stained,
Not with your sister's, but with your father's blood.

Amphilocus

What?

Alcmaeon

    I gave my twins to a friend of mine
Who swore to me that she'd take care of them.
But this friend lied.

Amphilocus

    But which friend? Who?

Alcmaeon

Here you are, and your sister, alive,
In spite of all Creusa contrived to do.

Amphilocus

Creusa? My mother?

Alcmaeon

    Do you know another?

Amphilocus

But then that means, if it's all true
We're also here in spite of you.

Alcmaeon

    But –

Amphilocus

Too concerned with your own troubles
To consider those more helpless than yourself.

Alcmaeon

Please, my son –

Amphilocus

    Your son?
Tell me then, why do people have children, father,
If they won't care for them in adversity?
You were dead to me before,
Why should I not kill you now?

Alcmaeon

No reason, no reason I can see.
I, your father killed my mother, now you kill me.

Pause.

Amphilocus

No, I will not kill you,
Your punishment is that you must live on,
With yourself, and take responsibility
For the family you forsook.
You shall meet 'your friend' this evening as arranged.
I have in mind a little strategy
To expose the fiction of this royal family,
And my stepmother, Creusa, and her cruel game.

Alcmaeon

Thank you, my son, but one last thing.

Amphilocus

What is it, father?

Pause.

Alcmaeon

What is your name?

Creon's palace.

*CREUSA enters followed by ISTHMIAS. She holds the
necklace of Harmonia.*

Creusa

In a place a million miles from here, she said?
And what type of work did she find fit for her?

Isthmias

A position in the service industries, she said.

Creusa

The work experience will do her good.
This pleases me enormously,
And the necklace rescued too,
And my place as queen of Corinth ensured!
This evening sees all my plans realised.
Isthmias, come dress me and paint my face,
I'll mask the crumbling temple of my looks,
With the semblance of the splendour I once was.

Who says women wield no power in our world?
Today I have gone to war, and tonight,
I shall return home in triumph.
I've one last debt to pay that bitch, the Pythoness
Who stole my Alcmaeon from me.
In return for the necklace of Harmonia,
I shall have him in my bed one last time.
Moderation, Isthmias, they always preach,
Too much of anything is bad for one.
Did they teach you this when you were young?

Isthmias

Excess is inversely proportional to success,
Mortals should not dress themselves as Gods.

Creusa

But, Isthmias, what they didn't tell you was
That you can never have too much revenge.
Revenge on Manto, revenge on Creon,
And just a little too on Alcmaeon.
So, tonight I shall dress as a God,
Tonight I'll wear the saffron of my youth
In which a girl first tastes the sweetness
Of the Goddess Aphrodite. Come dress me,
And fix it with a golden pin.

ISTHMIAS helps CREUSA into the dress.

And if one is to dress oneself as a God,
One needs suitably divine accessories.
Give me the necklace of Harmonia.

There's a knocking at the door.

Quick, Isthmias, close the necklace's clasp.

ISTHMIAS does so. CREUSA breaks away in pain.

Isthmias, you ass, you pinched my skin. I'm bleeding.
Clean it up, Isthmias! (*Calling.*) We are coming.
How do I look, Isthmias? Tell me.
Could I not pass for twenty-five or even twenty?

Isthmias

Experience has its attractions too.

Creusa

Men do not want experience for fear
It shows the limitations of their own.

There is another knock at the door.

Be calm Creusa, you are nearly home.

*Beat. CREUSA gestures ISTHMIAS to open door and turns
away, striking a pose.*

*ALCMAEON enters led by a slave:
AMPHILOCHUS. He is blind.
CREUSA does not turn for him.*

Thank you, Isthmias, that will be all.

Exit ISTHMIAS.

Alcmaeon, you kept your word and came.
And I've kept mine. I have what you came for.
But you'll have to remove it from my breast
With your own hands, as once you caressed,
When I was young and easily led, my body.
Gods, I loved you – I swore to myself that I would not say it,
But what does it matter now? – I'm giddy,
As if I'd drunk my wine undiluted.
I could drink you down, Alcmaeon.
I'm tired of wet and watery men.
I loved you, I would not have left you.
I saw us, all our future days, I saw them all.
Let me taste one of those days she stole from me.
Look, here is what you came for. Look, see.

*CREUSA turns to show necklace. She sees that ALCMAEON
is blind.*

Alcmaeon

When I came to Corinth I could see,
Yet did not know what I was looking for.
Once more I read an oracle literally,
The necklace was the key, but not the thing itself.
This is why the old women laughed at me
And taunted me and drove me so easily
From place to place and bed to bed.

And I preferred to run than stop and look
And see the woman in whose arms I lay.
They were all the same to me, until today.
In Corinth, city of my birth, that gave us
The word Korinthazomai, to fuck,
Up in the famous Temple of Aphrodite,
In the eyes of a young girl who stood there,
Shaking like a leaf, afraid of this man,
And what he wished to do with her, to her.
Yet, proudly, she did not retreat, or flinch,
But met my look, and in that look I saw,
Looking back at me, myself, standing there,
Shaking like a leaf, afraid, afraid of this man
And what he'd done, and what he still could do.
And not only did I see with her eyes,
Her eyes now seemed my eyes, the same bright blue,
That every woman whom I've ever had
Has told me are so striking and so dead.
But these eyes, that I saw in this girl, were alive,
No longer luring me, but lulling me to sleep.
And as I slept I had the strangest dream;
A boy, the image of this girl, came to me.
And, since he had my eyes too, he seemed
A younger me, except he had no fear,
And this boy then held a knife to my neck,
And whispered in my ear, he was my son,
Come back down from the mountain long ago,
Where he and his sister had been left to die.
And his sister, this girl, whom I now slept beside,
Whom I had so nearly korinthiazomaied.
And I saw, for the first time, I saw that it was them,
And not some necklace, made by a jealous God,
I had been looking for all this time.
I opened my eyes to look at her, my child,
And found this girl who had my eyes,
Had had my eyes, and I was blind.
Though strange to say, Creusa, in blindness,
I now see things as they really are and were.

Creusa

You're blind and foolish, Alcmaeon. Aren't you ashamed
To spin such yarns in the presence of a slave?

Alcmaeon

A slave must share his master's sufferings,
And this slave has borne more suffering than most.

Creusa

Since when have you cared for the suffering
Of any person but yourself?

Alcmaeon

Since this slave gave me certain proofs this girl
Was, in fact, who my dream had said she was.

Creusa

Your daughter died on a mountain years ago.
And the man who trusts a slave's word is a fool, Alcmaeon.

Alcmaeon

But what about the man who trusts his son?

The slave is revealed as AMPHILOCHUS.

Creusa

What is this I'm looking at?

Amphilocus

The truth of your actions, Creusa.

Alcmaeon

The son you told me was dead, Creusa.

Amphilocus

Whom you first raised as your own,
Then sold into slavery rather than see –

Creusa

Sold into slavery – ?

Amphilocus

– the web of lies you'd woven unravel.

Alcmaeon

Like a house built on sand it is unwise
To build a home upon foundation of lies.

Creusa

What is the point of truth if it then breaks
The very home the lies have helped to make?
I loved you, Alcmaeon, I would not have left you.
I saw us, all our future days, I saw them all,
The house, the home, the children, plenty,
And at the centre of it all, you and me.
Where is she? Where is Tisiphone?

Amphilocus

My sister whom you sold as a whore –

Creusa

A whore? Never. She was my daughter,
I only ever wanted to protect her.

Amphilocus

She is being washed and cared for
By the women of the Temple. Creon said –

Creusa

He knows?

Amphilocus

Of course, he had to know.

Creusa

Then I am dead.

Amphilocus

Creon said that he shall escort her home.

Creusa

And then escort her to my bed.
I saw us, all our future days, I saw them all,
But now I'm denied even one last taste
Of the dream you seduced me with back then.
No, nothing is so sweet as desire
Nectar from the most prized flower...
Isthmias! Isthmias!

ISTHMIAS enters.

Quick, to my room, I must pack.

Exit ISTHMIAS and CREUSA.

Amphilocus

Pack? Where are you going? You can't run away
From the justice that is due your actions.
Father, the door is locked, she will escape.

AMPHILOCHUS beats the door.

Where can you hope to run to? Who would shelter
A woman who has sold her son and daughter?
A woman who has deceived her husband,
Not only as to who his children were,
But who she secretly desired and planned
To lure into her viper's bed?

Alcmaeon

When you've lived and loved a little longer
You will see that life –

Amphilocus

What are you saying father?

Alcmaeon

I'm saying have compassion son.

The door gives way and opens.
AMPHILOCHUS hesitates, then exits.

Amphilocus

(*Off.*) Mother!

Banging on an interior door. CHORUS enter followed by
CREON and TISIPHONE.

Chorus

The weft is woven through the warp,
I push the shuttle back and forth,
My life lies stretched upon this loom,
This house of love shall be my tomb.

The banging of the interior door stops.

Creon

Where is the woman who would sell her child
Into a bondage worse than slavery,
Where is she? She shall face my justice and my wrath.

Enter ISTHMIAS

Isthmias

Creon, she is gone.

Creon

                She has escaped? Quick!
Send soldiers down each route from the city!
Then we shall have her stoned to death
And thrown from the highest rocks,
So the vultures, crows and dogs can feed on her;
The only use she is to any living thing.

Isthmias

Call back your men, Creon, they'll not find her there,
She is far beyond your jurisdiction,
And your justice which condemns us women –
Streetwalkers, slaves, and even those with social standing –
To be objects whose worth is weighed in whether we
Contribute to men's pleasure or posterity.
When I went with her to her room just now,
And watched her prepare for her final journey,
I remembered another journey that we made
To the mountains, some sixteen years ago.
You, Creon, were away at war,
The war at Thebes that had raged on
After blind Oedipus had gone into exile.
You had left her with an ultimatum
To perform her wifely duty and produce a child,
Or you would have her put to death.
And though she knew where the problem lay,
She was true to you and refused to lie,
Though I urged her to, with someone who
Might make up for your shortcomings.
Think what you like, Creon, I'm not afraid to die,
And I'll have my say before I do.

What courage I have gained Creusa's given me.
We had gone to the mountains, all those years ago;
A distant mountain range inland,
And with us, two babies, twins, a boy and girl,
Situated far from human habitation,
So no living soul would hear them cry,
Our purpose was to leave them there to die.
She'd promised their father, Alcmaeon,
Whom she loved more than herself,
Who, like their mother, had abandoned them,
'What kind of life can they expect? No home,
No family, no love and no respect?
Position is everything, they have none'
She knew what it was to be abandoned,
She knew what it was to live on the brink
Of obliteration from society.
So she'd sworn she would take care of them
And spare them from the sufferings of life.
Not that she wished to do this. No,
The very thought of it appalled her,
And when we had decided on the place,
My mistress asked me if I'd be the one
To leave them there, bound hand and foot.
I agreed, and she went back down the mountain.
I did the deed though could not look at them,
Then went and joined Creusa down below.
But when I reached her she told me to hush.
I listened and, in the stifling noonday silence,
A distant sound, like lambs trapped in a fence,
Bleating for their mothers to come to them.
In truth, I cried too and it was all that I could do
To stop myself from running back to rescue them.
But Creusa shed no tears, in fact she smiled;
'Little twin born beams of light,
You have been consumed by the mountain sun,
Gathered up into the golden chariot
Of Apollo, there to shine down on us.
Isthmias, the children of Alcmaeon are dead.
But the sun God Apollo heals as well as destroys,

And in their stead he's left me two children of my own.
Listen, can't you hear them? They sound like lambs
Who have been separated from their flock.
Let us go take them out of this harsh light,
My own children, whom I shall feed and clothe,
And love, and give my life for, all my life.'
And when I went to her quarters just now,
She reminded me of what she'd said,
And how those two only lived because of her.
The light of Apollo that had blinded her, now dimmed,
She saw quite clearly what she had to do.
She bid me lay out her wedding linen,
Kneeled down in the middle of her bed and said;
'My wedding bed, garden of my hopes,
Now overrun with lies, choked with regrets,
Farewell sun whose harsh light I have known.'
Then, with trembling hands, she pulled from her dress
The golden pin, her arm and breast bared,
And as her own harsh son burst into the room,
She drove the pin, through the golden necklace,
The necklace of Harmonia, home into her heart.
Her son reached her as she fell dead into his arms.
He had heard all she said before she died,
And there he now cries for her, unreservedly.
His joy on finding his true father fades
At the death of the only mother he has known.
And there now I shall go. I've heard it said
A slave must share her mistress' sufferings.
I too must lie upon my mistress' bed.
So Women of Corinth come follow me,
And don't let faint heartedness hold you back,
You must see that our bodies are given
The due rites and respect we've lacked in life.

Chorus

The wind blows through the house,
The wind blows down the hall,
The cinders in the fireplace dance,
Shadows on a moonlit wall.

Death and desire walk hand in hand,
The lost loom up before our eyes,
The present is a haunted land,
In a home built on lies.

Exit CHORUS.

Creon

By what strange circuity of cruelty
And misfortune have we come to this conclusion.
Unhappy children who lost a mother,
Unhappy way to find a father too,
Unhappy Creusa, most unhappy who
Out of love and desire, and last out of despair –
No I'm not without blame in this affair –
Lived a lie, till that one lie led to another,
Until nothing in our house was what it seemed to be,
And as a consequence, unhappy me.
Only this evening, Alcmaeon, I told you
Of my daughter Tisiphone how she
Was the light that lit my day, but she was more.
My ears listened for her every step,
I watched her every inconsequential
Flick and skip and laugh and smile.
I ate them up. I wanted her so much it hurt.
And thinking her my daughter, thought myself
Unnatural, abnormal, worse than animal.
I could not bear to think that any man might touch her.
Yet, as her father, prayed that someone such as you,
Might marry her and remove her from my sight.
If you could only see her, I said, you'd see.
And you did see her, and now it is me,
Who, by this strange circuity of cruelty
And misfortune, asks you, now her father, and my friend,
If this unhappy story, might have a happy end.

Alcmaeon

Creon, once more I find myself in your debt
For raising, however unawares, my children.
But since the day that I gave them away,
And drove off in my chariot to Thebes,

91

I've lost whatever right I might have had,
To decide upon their future happiness.
Besides, you have brought them up so well and wise
That Tisiphone herself can advise you
Whether she grants or denies you your request.

Creon

Tisiphone, what do you say?
I know it is an old cliché,
But you would make this old cliché beam,
If you would consent to be his queen.

Tisiphone

Sir, the throne is still warm from your last,
Besides I've seen enough of the pleasures
Of the unwalked way today, my old cliché,
I wish to stay upon more beaten tracks.
Therefore must forego the chance to be your wife.

Creon

What? This is no way to end a story.

Tisiphone

Is real life not like that? Unsatisfactory?

Creon

Real life? I am the King and I have all these feelings –
I demand a God come crashing through the ceiling.

Pause.

Alcmaeon

The Gods are long dead, they have abandoned us.

Enter HERA through the ceiling.

Hera

No, we have not abandoned you,
We have just grown older, tireder,
Less time and more things to do.

Pause. She looks around. She clears her throat.

I am golden-throned Hera, whom Rhea bore,
Queen of the Immortals, I surpass all

In wisdom and in beauty. Wife and sister to
Loud thundering Zeus – yes,
We have our dysfunction too –
Nor would I be slandering him to say
My husband/brother is a philanderer
On an altogether different scale.
But, in recognition of my suffering,
My fellow Gods have appointed me
Protectress of the family.
One does one's best to make amends,
Put something back, in the hope, no doubt forlorn,
That the sins of our fathers remain just that,
Their sins, and not pollute the family as a whole.
But hope is an elusive flower,
It sustains us in our darkest hour,
Then withers once we are through the storm.
Alcmaeon, in recognising your family
You have laid to rest the Erinyes,
The avengers of your mother.
Though you shall remain blind,
You shall return to your wife Callirhoe
With the necklace of Harmonia,
As you promised that you would.
Unfortunately, your second wife,
Alphesiboea of Psophis,
Will claim it's hers by rights, and not the third's.
Her father, Phegeus, will claim your life,
For this Callirhoe shall swear undying enmity,
And so shall continue the circuity of internecine strife
Begun by this necklace at Thebes.
First Harmonia, then Jocasta,
Then your mother, Eriphyle.
This necklace has only ever brought bad luck
But greed blinds human beings
To the wickedness that it contains.
Creon, you shall marry Tisiphone.
Apollo's oracle said she must lie with her father,
And though I'd rather not do this to you, child,
Oracles must in some way come true,

Else what would become of me and you?
And your father by upbringing's the best that I can do.
Nor does the 'circuity' of suffering end here;
She shall give you a child of your own,
Glauke, the silver-eyed or owl-eyed,
But in giving birth to whom, she shall die.
Broken-hearted you shall finally see
The greatest Goddess is not Aphrodite, but me,
And found The Temple of Hera Bounaia
Where Tisiphone shall be laid in perpetuity.
En passant, Glauke, your child, shall also die,
Poisoned by a dress on her wedding day,
Given to her by her husband's first wife,
A foreigner by the name of Medea.
You'll die too, Creon, trying to aid her.
Finally, Amphilochus, where is he?

Tisiphone

With his mother, shall I go get him?

Hera

Yes.
No. There's not the time, I must be getting on.
Just tell him that from Corinth he must go north,
To a place upon the Ambracian Gulf,
And there he must plant his sword
And found the town of Amphilochean Argos.

Tisiphone

And this new city shall be a place of hope?

Hera

Unlikely, but I suppose there's a chance.
Which brings me finally to the ants.

All

The ants?

Hera

Briefly, under the heat of a benevolent sun
An ant crawled from the crack or hole,
Where he had cowered all winter long.

And he looked up towards the heavens,
And, thinking himself blessed, busied himself
Building on earth the shapes he had seen in the sky.
And when he'd done, he looked at what he'd built.
And he thought it most mighty and most marvellous.
And called it a city, and he thought himself a God
For the making of this trifling thing.
And he ruled over it with a rod of iron.
But then the sun's light grew more harsh and slanted,
The wind picked up and unplucked the threads
From which his world was woven,
Till nothing but a few fragments remained,
Snatches of sentences on dusty leaves
Torn from old book rolls…
And he went back down the crack or hole,
And curled up, and waited for the sun to shine again.

Creon

Which is all supposed to show?

Hera

Enjoy the brief light of the sun,
It is all, then the darkness comes.

> *Exit HERA. Enter the Chorus with the bodies of CREUSA*
> *and ISTHMIAS.*

Chorus

The Gods are always near us
They walk beside us,
Though seldom hear us.
Walk with us now and cheer us.

The End.

www.ingramcontent.com/pod-product-compliance
Ingram Content Group UK Ltd.
Pitfield, Milton Keynes, MK11 3LW, UK
UKHW020724280225
455688UK00012B/494